THE ADVENTURES OF THE FLYING ABUELITA

LAS ADVENTURAS DE LA ABUELITA VOLADORA

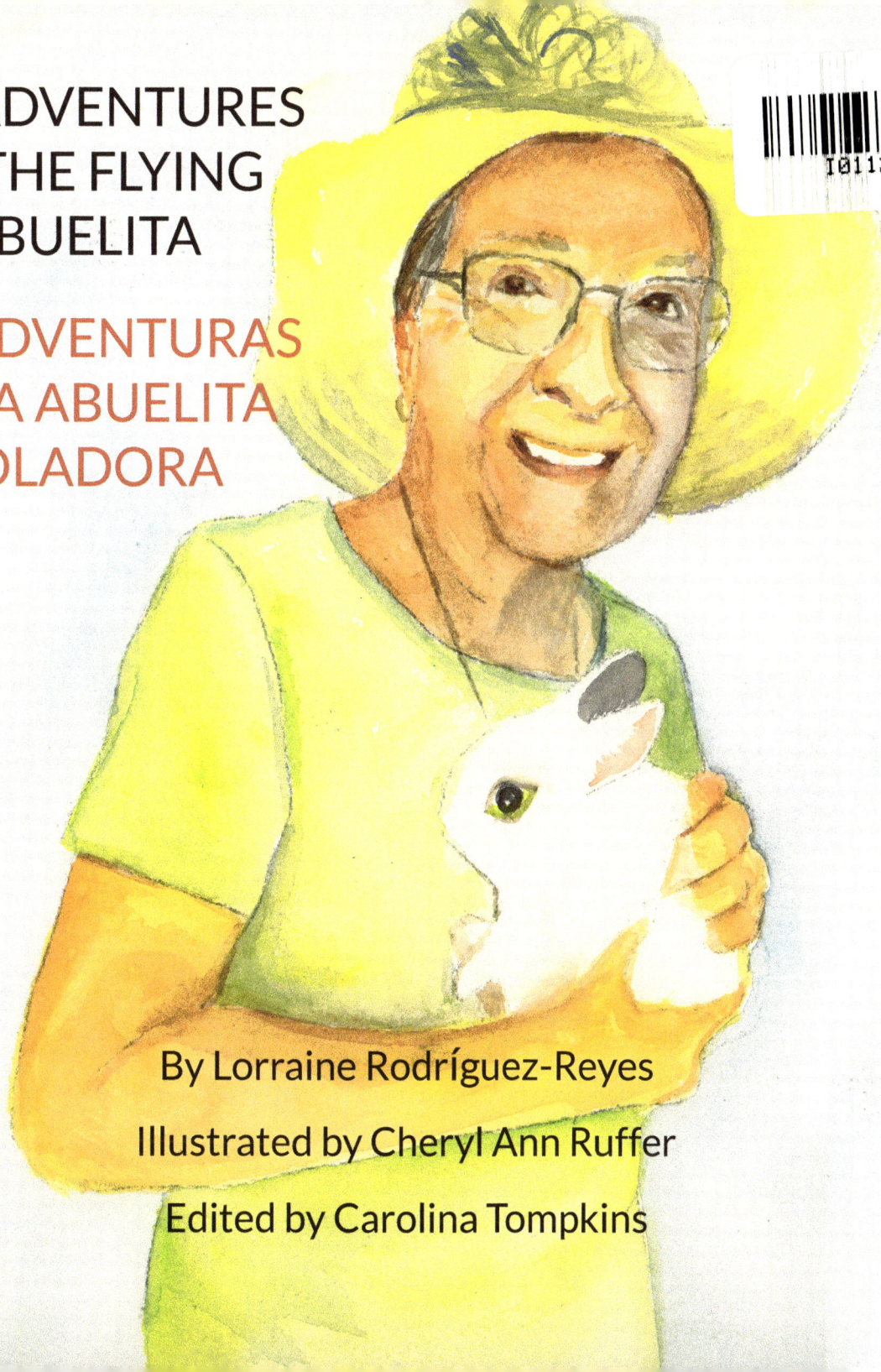

By Lorraine Rodríguez-Reyes

Illustrated by Cheryl Ann Ruffer

Edited by Carolina Tompkins

© Copyright 2024 Lorraine Rodríguez-Reyes
The Adventures of the Flying Abuelita

Published by Yawn's Publishing
2555 Marietta Hwy, Ste 103
Canton, GA 30114
www.yawnsbooks.com

Library of Congress Control Number: 2024927101

ISBN: 978-1-954617-97-1 Paperback
        978-1-954617-98-8 Hardcover

Printed in the United States

Dedication:

To Mami, a wonderful Abuelita who inspires and encourages us to dream big and always find our new adventure. We love you!

Dedicatoria:

A Mami, una Abuelita maravillosa que nos inspira y anima a soñar en grande y encontrar nuevas aventuras. ¡Te amamos!

Once there was a beautiful couple named Ito and Abuelita. They used to dance, sail on cruise ships, and they loved to discover new places. One day Ito got sick, and he knew he had to go on his own journey. Before he left, he told Abuelita, "It's time for you to go on your own adventure. I have to go to heaven." Abuelita became a widow.

Había una pareja llamada Ito y Abuelita. Ellos bailaban, viajaban, paseaban en cruceros y les encantaban descubrir nuevos lugares. Un día Ito se enfermó y sabía que ya era hora de comenzar su propia aventura solo. Antes de irse, le dijo a Abuelita, "Llegó la hora de que continúes con tu propia aventura. Me tengo que ir al cielo."
Asi fue como Abuelita se quedó viuda.

Life wasn't the same without Ito. Abuelita missed dancing with him and hearing his funny jokes that made her laugh till her belly hurt. She tried to keep busy, but she was still very lonely.

La vida no era igual sin Ito. Abuelita extrañaba bailar con él y escuchar sus chistes divertidos que la hacían reír a carcajadas. Ella intentaba distraerse, pero se sentía muy sola.

One day Abuelita had an idea: "I can go live with my daughter, son-in-law and grandchildren. Then I won't be lonely, and they will bring me joy." So, Abuelita packed up her treasures and moved in with her family. Soon she was flying all over town, going to her events and helping with her grandchildren.

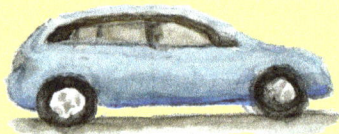

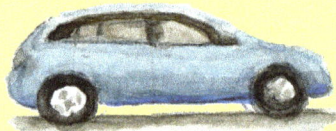

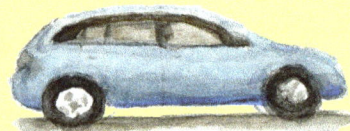

Un día Abuelita tuvo una idea: "Puedo ir a vivir con mi hija, mi yerno, y mis nietos. Así no me sentiré tan sola y ellos me traerán mucha alegría." Abuelita empaco sus tesoros y se mudó con su familia. Pronto volaba por toda la ciudad yendo a sus eventos y ayudando con sus nietos.

Abuelita laughed and played with her grandchildren. Their crazy antics kept her really busy.

Abuelita se reía y jugaba con sus nietos; se divertían muchísimo. Las locuras de sus nietos la mantenía bien ocupadita.

She cooked with her daughter. She played bingo with her friends and dominos with the family. On Sundays Abuelita went to Church and brunch.

Ella cocinaba con su hija. Jugaba bingo con sus amistades y dominós con la familia. Los domingos, Abuelita iba a la iglesia y almorzaba con sus amigas.

But every once in
a while she cried in
the supermarket.
She was still lonely.
Abuelita had very
big feelings.

Pero, de vez en cuando ella se encontraba llorando en el
supermercado. Ella se sentía muy sola. Abuelita tenía unos
sentimientos muy grandes.

Abuelita really missed Ito and their adventures together. She missed hearing him laugh and tell his very funny jokes.

Abuelita extrañaba muchísimo a Ito y las aventuras que disfrutaban juntos. Ella añoraba la risa de Ito y sus chistes tan divertidos.

One day her daughter asked, "Are you ok, Mami? You seem really sad." Abuelita quietly replied, "I'm OK." But her daughter knew better. She turned to Abuelita and said, "Let's go on an adventure. Let's try something new! Come with me to a Tai Chi and Qi Gong class." "What is Tai Chi and Qi Gong?" Abuelita asked. "Just wait and see", her daughter replied, smiling. "It's part of the adventure."

Un día su hija le preguntó, "¿Estás bien, Mami? Te noto muy triste." Abuelita respondió con voz sombría, "Si. Estoy bien." Pero su hija sabía que algo no estaba bien. "¡Vamos a embarcar en una aventura y hacer algo nuevo! Ven conmigo a tomar unas clases de Tai Chi y Chi Kung." "¿Qué es eso?", preguntó Abuelita. "Espera y verás", le contestó su hija sonriendo. "Es parte de la aventura."

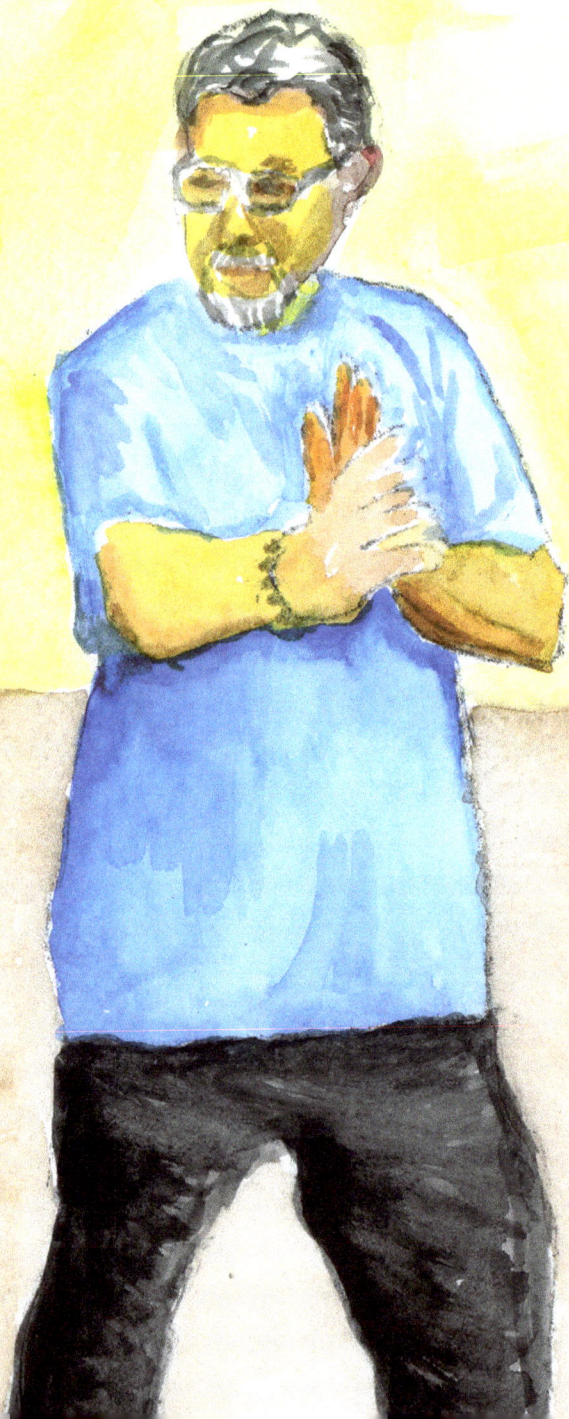

A couple of days later, her daughter took Abuelita to a Tai Chi and Qi Gong class. The teacher was called Shifu. He was very patient and kind. Abuelita learned all the choreographed movements. She really wished Ito was there taking these classes with her. They would have laughed a lot!

Unos días después, su hija llevó a Abuelita a clases de Tai Chi y Chi Kung. El maestro se llamaba Shifu. Él era muy paciente y amable. Abuelita aprendió todos los movimientos coreografiados de Tai Chi y Chi Kung. Ella tenía un deseo muy grande de compartir estas clases con Ito. ¡Ellos se hubiesen reído muchísimo!

At the end of class Shifu said, "I would like to invite all of you to my daughter Maria's ranch in Brazil called Lar Horse. There, you will meet other people who practice Tai Chi and Qi Gong as well."

For the first time in a long time Abuelita's eyes lit up like stars. She thought about the promise she made to Ito before he went to heaven, and turning to her daughter she said, "Let's go on an adventure!"

Al final de la clase Shifu dijo, "Los quiero invitar a la finca de mi hija Maria en Brasil; se llama Lar Horse. Allí van a conocer más personas que practican Tai Chi y Chi Kung."

Los ojos de Abuelita brillaban como las estrellas, algo que no había sucedido por mucho tiempo. Abuelita pensó en la promesa que le hizo a Ito antes de que él se fuera al cielo. Miró a su hija y exclamó, "¡Vámonos de aventura!"

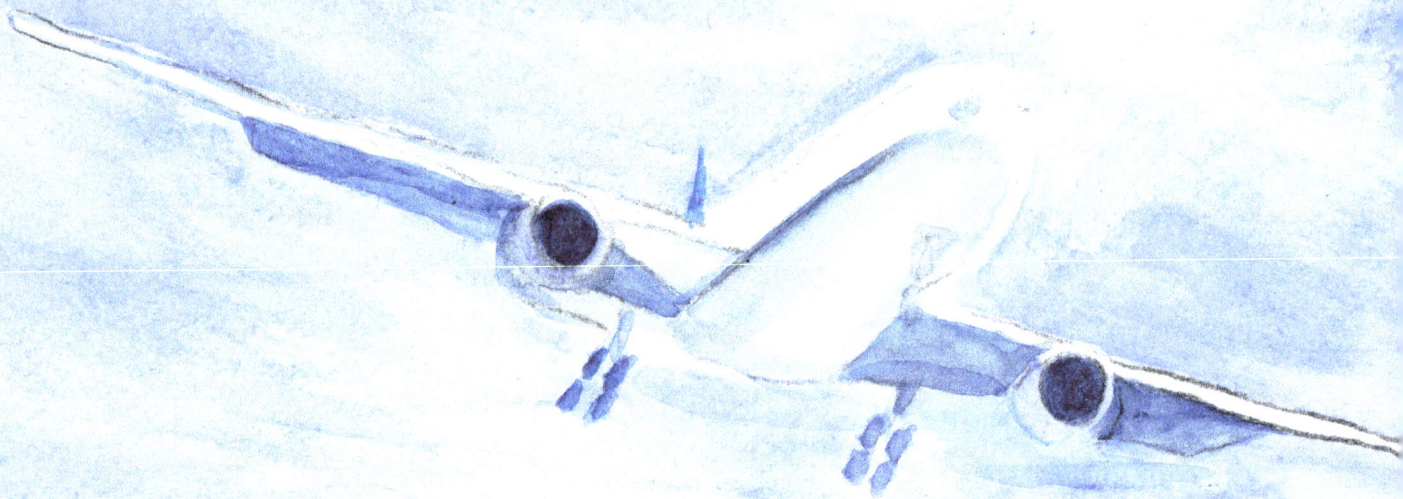

A few weeks later, Abuelita and her daughter took a flight from Atlanta, Georgia in the United States to São Paulo, Brazil. The journey took ten hours!

Unas semanas después, Abuelita y su hija volaron en avión de Atlanta, Georgia en los Estados Unidos a São Paulo, Brasil. ¡El viaje duró diez horas!

ATL

BRAZIL

Abuelita was exhausted when she got off the plane. But she smiled when she saw Maria, Shifu's daughter. "Welcome to Brazil!", Maria exclaimed. "Don't get too comfy because we still have a four-hour drive to my ranch, Lar Horse." Abuelita didn't care. When she bounced around in the car as they drove through bumpy roads, she pretended she was on a rollercoaster. She was giddy with excitement to start her new adventure!

Cuando el avión aterrizó, Abuelita estaba exhausta. Pero tan pronto vio a Maria, la hija de Shifu, le sonrió con una sonrisa grande y bella. "¡Bienvenidos a Brasil!", exclamó Maria. "No se acomoden mucho porque todavía nos faltan cuatro horas de camino para llegar a mi finca Lar Horse." Pero a Abuelita no le importó. Cuando el carro brincaba mientras conducían por las calles llenas de huecos, Abuelita pretendía estar montada en una montaña rusa. ¡Estaba muy emocionada por comenzar su nueva aventura!

Finally they arrived at Lar Horse. Abuelita and her daughter were staying at a horse farm!

At Lar Horse, Abuelita did things she never imagined.

Por fin llegaron a Lar Horse. ¡Abuelita y su hija se iban a quedar en una finca de caballos!

En Lar Horse, Abuelita hizo cosas que jamás hubiese imaginado.

She learned how to meditate. That is when we sit quietly and focus on our senses. Abuelita was having difficulty concentrating. Her mind sometimes wanted to go on its own adventure. Shifu taught her a trick. "Focus on one word and your mind will become quieter."

Aprendió a meditar. Meditar es cuando nos sentamos en silencio para concentrarnos en nuestros sentidos. Abuelita tenía mucha dificultad concentrándose. Su mente quería ir en su propia aventura. Shifu le enseñó un truco. "Enfócate en una palabra y verás que tu mente se tranquiliza."

Every morning Abuelita practiced Tai Chi and Qi Gong on the deck overlooking the beautiful mountains. The graceful movements made Abuelita feel calm. It helped her with her big emotions.

Cada mañana Abuelita practicaba Tai Chi y Chi Kung en una plataforma con la vista más bella de las montañas. Los movimientos delicados fueron calmando y tranquilizando a Abuelita. Le ayudaron con sus grandes emociones.

Abuelita went on a hike for the very first time. Everyone said, "That is so AMAZING for an 84-year-old Abuelita!" During the hike, Abuelita met the horses. Did you know that horses can feel our emotions? Abuelita didn't know, but she learned.

Abuelita hizo una caminata por primera vez. Todos dijeron, "¡Que MARAVILLOSO para una Abuelita de 84 años!" Durante la caminata, Abuelita se encontró con los caballos. ¿Sabían que los caballos pueden sentir nuestras emociones? Abuelita no lo sabía, pero lo aprendió.

One day, a pony called Estrella kept nudging Abuelita. Not only can horses feel our emotions, but they make connections with us too. Estrella LOVED Abuelita! Abuelita was the only one Estrella allowed to pet and ride her. Abuelita and Estrella became friends. Wherever Abuelita went, Estrella followed.

Un día, un poni llamada Estrella no dejaba de empujar a Abuelita. Los caballos no solo pueden sentir nuestras emociones, sino que también crean conexiones con nosotros. Estrella AMABA a Abuelita. Abuelita era la única a quien Estrella permitía acariciarla y montar en ella. Abuelita y Estrella se hicieron amigas. Donde quiera que iba Abuelita, Estrella la seguía.

On the last day of the trip, Abuelita had her biggest adventure yet–she went on a night hike! She put her headlamp on, grabbed her walking sticks and, with Shifu's help, ventured out into the night.

En el último día del viaje, Abuelita tuvo la aventura más asombrosa de su vida. Agarró sus bastones de paseo, una linterna y, con la ayuda de Shifu, ¡se desafío hacer una caminata nocturna!

During the hike there were times when Abuelita was scared. It was dark. The ground was muddy and hilly. But, with Ito in her heart, she kept putting one foot in front of the other. Soon she made it to the bonfire. There she found the rest of her campmates. Everyone was singing and dancing. Abuelita joined in and started rapping, something she had never done before! She was named "The Abuelita Rapper".

Durante la caminata, hubo momentos en que Abuelita tenía miedo. La noche estaba oscura. El camino era montañoso y lleno de lodo. Pero, con Ito en su corazón, Abuelita siguió paso a paso hasta que logró llegar a la fogata. Allí se encontró con el resto de sus compañeros. Todos estaban cantando y bailando. Abuelita se unió a ellos y empezó a rapear, ¡algo que jamás había hecho! La nombraron "La Abuelita Rapera".

Before Abuelita started the long journey home, she looked out over Lar Horse and smiled. As she gazed up at heaven, she whispered, "Dear Ito, I kept my promise."

Antes de comenzar el largo viaje a casa, Abuelita miró hacia Lar Horse y sonrió. Volteando su mirada al cielo, susurro, "Querido Ito, cumplí con mi promesa."

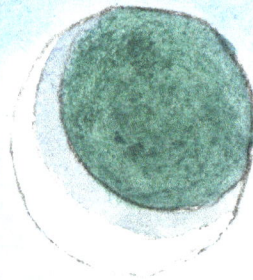

On her way home Abuelita was already planning her next adventure. "Rome seems like a nice place to visit", she thought. "I can learn Italian, too!"

The End ... for now!

Regresando a casa Abuelita ya estaba ideando su próxima aventura. "Roma sería un lindo lugar para visitar", pensó. "¡Hasta podría aprender italiano!"

El Fin... por ahora!

Follow in Abuelita's footsteps and go on your own adventure!

"We are expressions of the Source, living a human experience on this beautiful planet, in a deep communion with the Eternal."
Shifu Efrain Brady

Sigue el ejemplo de Abuelita y ¡embarca en tu propia aventura!

"Todos somos una expresión del Universo. Vivimos la experiencia humana en este hermoso planeta en profunda comunión con el Eterno."
Shifu Efrain Brady

With Love & Appreciation:

I would like to express my deepest appreciation and love to my husband Marc for listening to all my crazy ideas and supporting them. For my children Marcus Joaquín and Julia Helena, you keep me on my toes and my imagination alive. Maria Diaz-Hudson, my best friend, thank you for all your support, love and for reading this story countless times via text. Thank you for always being happy for my happiness. Farrah Haidar, my creative sister who always says "YES AND". Thank you for giving me writing tutorials. You are an Excellent teacher! Maegan Flynn, Kristen Golub and Marco Antonio Rodriguez thank you for encouragement, feedback and support.

La Familia Cairo and the cousins Bayoán, Yuiza, Kymani, Nozai and Anani, thank you for listening to the book and giving me your honest feedback. You guys inspire me, and we always look forward to our adventures together.

To my editor and friend Carolina Tompkins, your faith, love and support throughout this process has been invaluable. Thank you for constantly checking on me, the long conversations, the shared google docs, revisions and cafecitos! I look forward to our next adventure together.

Shifu Efrain Brady, Maria, Oscar and Israel at Lar House. Working with all of you has been magical! My spirit is full. Cheryl, my talented illustrator, what a blessing it was to take this journey with you.

Thank you Nadine and Farris from Yawn Publishing for your patience and guidance; and helping my dreams come true.

Aida Luz Rodríguez "Abuelita" resides in Johns Creek, GA with her Daughter, Son-in-law, and her grandchildren Marcus Joaquín and Julia Helena. Abuelita loves traveling and being of service to those in need.

Lorraine is an actress and teaches part-time at Georgia State University residing in Johns Creek, GA with her husband, children and mother.

It was amazing to meet Lorraine and her mom Aida on our adventure at Lar Horse in Brazil. I am honored to have been asked to illustrate this tribute to a remarkable woman. Painting with watercolor (aquarella in Spanish) was a challenge as I am predominantly an oil painter.

My husband and I reside in Cherokee County, GA. It's been a great place to have raised our son and daughter and after 21 years here we transplants now think of it as home.

I consider it my job to put beauty and love into the world with my art. Fortunately, I have abundant support from family and friends to accomplish this goal.

www.ingramcontent.com/pod-product-compliance
Lightning Source LLC
LaVergne TN
LVHW070841080426

835513LV00024B/2428